Clean it Best #20 Cleaning Tips Second Edition

DB Creative Brand & Consulting Publishing
South Bend, Indiana
www.dorlitablakely.com

ISBN: 9798734606612 Paperback
Printed in the United States of America

Clean it Best #20 Cleaning Tips

Second Edition
by Stephanie Wilson

Table of Contents

lean It
Best

About Stephanie Wilson

I got started in the business by talking to my husband. He told me to think about it, and I did for the first week. I was back and forth about it. I decided to give it a try and see how it would be. I didn't expect the outcome to be so good with me getting clients and starting a partnership. Still, I did, and it was a fantastic start for me.

The persons that said I should open my business and gave me the ideas were my sister-in-law and my husband. They said, "I loved to clean so why not do it for a living." They have always told me that I was good at what I was doing and that I should make a business out of it.

I started my business because it was something that I had always dreamed of doing, owning my own business. Even though I didn't know what I wanted to do owning a business was right in my face the whole time. One day I became strong and confident enough to start my own cleaning business. I fulfill a lifelong dream that I had since I was a child. To be able to work for myself. And that is what I did.

-Stephanie Wilson

This book is dedicated to my husband, Shelby. He believed in me and gave me the idea to open my own business. He has been with me throughout this entire process.

Tip #1

How to get rid of soap scum . . .

Get your supplies non-scratch pad, you can get this from any Dollar Store or Walmart. You will also need degreaser or all-purpose cleaner. I like to use Lysol or MeanGreen.

You can get these products from me, any Menards or Home Depot for $3.00 or less. Your choice or you can mix vinegar with water. Clorox bleach and terry cloth towel.

Spray it down all around the tub. You don't need much just enough so it's wet.

Grab your SOS pad or non-scratch pad and start scrubbing along the tub.

Last step after you gotten all the soap scum off (yes, I finally did it). Get your clean towel with some Clorox bleach and wipe it down good. Then you're all done, you've gotten all the soap scum.

Tip #2

How to clean hardwood flooring...

You can get this mop from Family Dollar or even Amazon for $15.00. Also, a dry terry cloth or towel and a floor duster.

My Favorite brand is Dirt Devil,

NO VACCUM (it may scratch your floors). Once you have everything, go to the next step.

Begin by dusting or sweeping the floors (NO STEAMERS they will make hardwood floors buckle)

Start from top to bottom when cleaning floors

Make sure your mop is damp. Water is hardwood floors nightmare so make sure it's a damp mop.

Then go ahead and start mopping to get a good clean, safe hardwood shine!

Don't use any oils or waxes, lemon juice vinegar on your floors, (it will damage your floors and seals. Try ¼ cup of mild soap into the water. Dawn is a very good soap to use.

Tip #3

How to clean a car seat properly…

Get the stain as soon as it spills. Faster results are more successful.

Check the car seat manual. It may have some tips, if not that's ok.

Get your supplies, soft towel, sponge, Dirt Devil vacuum (handheld) is very good to use or a Shark vacuum. Warm water, gentle soap (Dawn)

Wipe off what you can using the vacuum or towel.

Remove the padding. Most padding can go in the washing machine under delicate wash

With mild soap (I use purėx its good for people with sensitive skin) DO NOT PUT IN DRYER!!!!

Clean the harness and buckles (do not use heavy duty cleaners)

After you are done air dry padding before you put it back in the seat.

Tip #4

How to clean stainless steel...

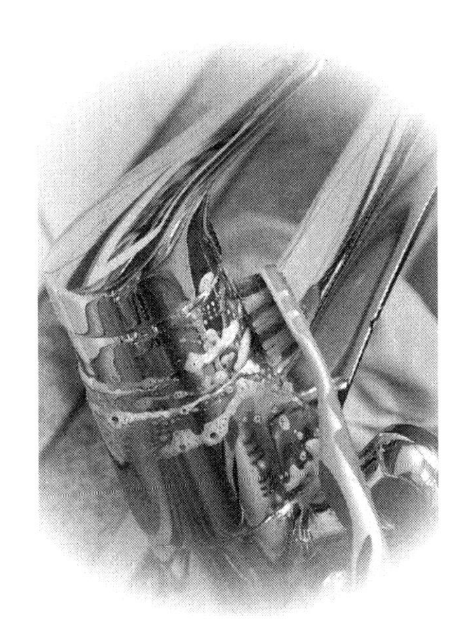

Get mild detergent (dawn), 2 soft towels, baking soda, and a sponge toothbrush for tough spots and warm water.

Dip a soft cloth in warm water mixed with mild detergent.

Wipe the surface then rinse the cloth and wipe again

Dry with a dry towel

To remove baked on food and grease, use warm water and baking soda in a bucket

Rub onto the surface using a sponge

Wipe with a wet towel then dry.

For scratches apply a stainless-steel cleaner. I like to use Spray way brands that leave it shiny and clean.

Tip #5

How to remove rust from your oven...

Grab your towel, bottle of Coca-Cola (24oz), non-scratch pad.

Pour the Coca-Cola over the rust or use a sponge and pour Coca-Cola on it (for bigger jobs get a bin and pour Coca-Cola into it and let it sit overnight

Use a non-scratch pad to remove the remaining rust

After 15 minutes use a non-scratch pad or foil it may take a few seconds to get it off

Wipe clean with oven cleaner or just warm water.

Tip #6

How to remove streaks from glass windows...

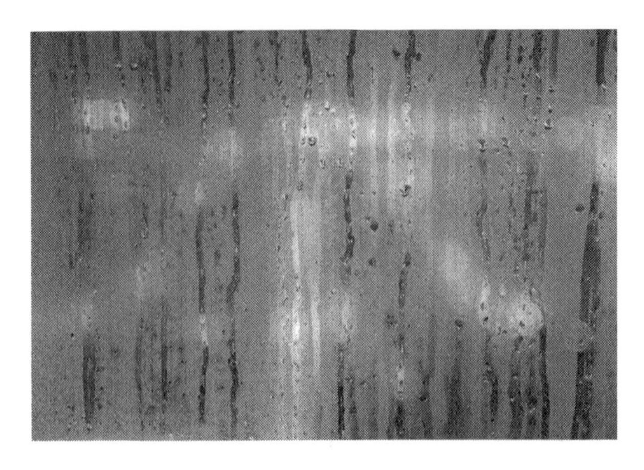

You will need vinegar, non-scratch pad or razor, sponge you can get all these items from the Dollar Stores or Walmart, vacuum (Dirt Devil), squeegee, towels and Spin Mop bucket.

Remove stains and grime from the windows with white vinegar. Let it sit for 2 minutes before wiping

Use a handheld vacuum and vacuum the windows. Towels and sponges can collect dust and end up leaving streaks when you are about to wipe the window dry.

Mix your supplies vinegar (1 tablespoon) and water.

Scrub your windows with the sponge.

Wipe the windows dry with the squeegee, make sure you wipe the blade off after every swipe.

Tip #7

How to clean shower glass doors...

Grab 2 or more towels, non-scratch pad, your invisible cleaner is a good glass cleaner (vinegar, water is the best)

Spray the glass down with the glass cleaner.

Get your non scratch pad and scrub your glass (wipe to see what is coming off to make sure you get it all

Wipe off all the scum.

Use your glass cleaner to get a brand-new shine

Tip #8

How to clean baseboards properly...

All you will need are three (3) towels two (2) dry and one (1) damp, toothbrush, bucket with warm water and add some Mr. Clean for a nice smell

Wet your towel and your toothbrush

Go across with your dry towel to get the cobwebs and dusties or you can use a swifter, they are very good.

Go across the top of the baseboard with your toothbrush using a back, and forth motion

After you have brushed your baseboards wipe down with a wet down

Then after you are all finished, dry them with your other dry towel then you have clean baseboards.

Tip #9

Carpet stains! How to get them out...

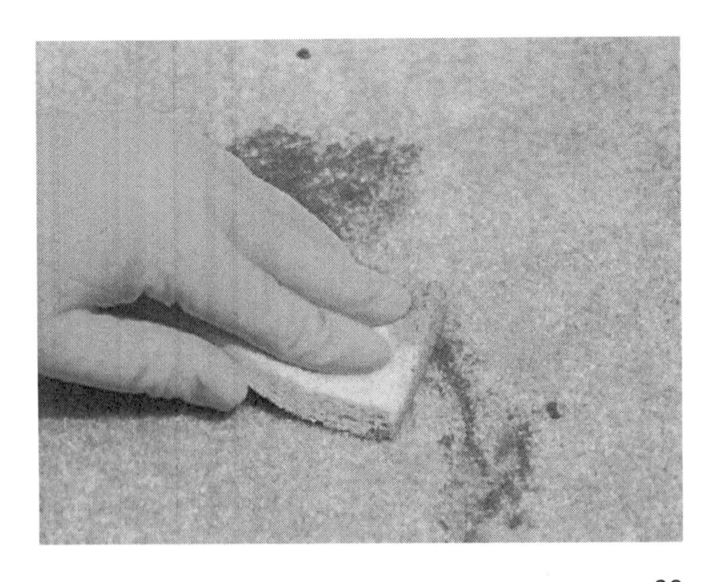

All you'll need is a sponge, towel, 1 tbsp. of dawn soap, ¼ tsp. of white vinegar, and a spray bottle.

Mix all of it together in your bottle with some water

Spray it on the stain in the carpet (soak it up)

Let it sit for 5 to 10 minutes

Then start blotting at the stain with your sponge until it's removed.

The Ultimate List of

Preventing Rust

How To:

Prevent rusting. All the objects in the bathroom that are made of metal start rusting after some time. The smell of rusting metal is the worst. I personally hate it a lot! In order to remove the rusted metal, I spray some WD-40 on them. It is very effective on metals. Then I apply transparent nail polish wherever possible. This creates a protective layer on the metal object so that it is not exposed to the air and water, hence preventing it from getting rust again. Apply a thin layer of nail paint on a monthly basis for the best result.

Tip #10

How to Remove Handprints from Your Wall...

Grab a towel, bucket with water, orange cleaner, or you can use Dawn soap and water, whatever you prefer.

Fill the bucket with water

After you have done that wet your towel in the bucket

Wipe your walls down (you may have to scrub just a little) the stain will come out

Your walls are looking clean again and remember that all stains will not always comes out. I would just get some primer and some white paint or whatever color you would like.

Tip #11

How to clean your home in 10 minutes before the company arrives...

For when you have just 10 minutes to spare: Flip the cushions on the couch so they don't see your stains the night before, wipe down all the counters and clear the table off. Straighten up the dining room chairs if you need to.

If you have a dishwasher put your dirty dishes in the dishwasher. After you are done light some candles in random areas of your home (where your company will be). Start cooking dinner. A fast quick meal so they will think you were busy cooking this whole time.

By the time they ring the doorbell, Surprise!!! It smells good, the food is halfway done, and the place doesn't look a mess. Great job done!!!!

Tip #12

No vacuum, what to do? Do this. 3 ways to clean your carpet...

1. Pick up small debris with a carpet sweeper. They are affordable tools and do not need power to use them.

2. Sweep your carpet or rug with a broom. They work better than a vacuum in my opinion. I recommend you use one that has bristles on the end.

3. Sprinkle the carpet with powder to cut odors, baking soda, cornstarch or pet odor powder will work fine.

Tip #13

How to clean wood blinds… Naturally

First, open the blinds and dust each slat using a non-abrasive cloth or duster.

Next, use a vacuum to remove any dust that has accumulated on some of the other blinds.

Your next step will depend on the type of material your blinds are made of. If your blinds are made of aluminum, vinyl or faux wood, they can be washed with a mixture of gentle antibacterial soap and water.

Dunk a cloth in the water and wipe down one slat at a time starting at the top and working your way down. If you have fabric shades or blinds, you should avoid washing them and simply spot clean any areas where there may be dirt. Never use water to clean wood blinds at all. Instead, regularly clean them with a dry cloth or vacuum.

Final step when cleaning your blinds:

Make sure to clean the pull strings, as these can easily be discolored by dust, dirt and sun damage. Dip a white cloth in a mixture of warm water and a fabric-safe cleaning solution and use this to grip the strings and move down the strings.

Tip #14

Did you spill red wine? Don't worry we got you covered...

Mix about 3 parts of hydrogen peroxide and 1 part of Dawn dish soap.

Apply to red wine carpet stain

Let it sit for 20 minutes to an hour

Then blot clean before attempting to fully wash out mixture.

Tip #15

Covid-19 Tips

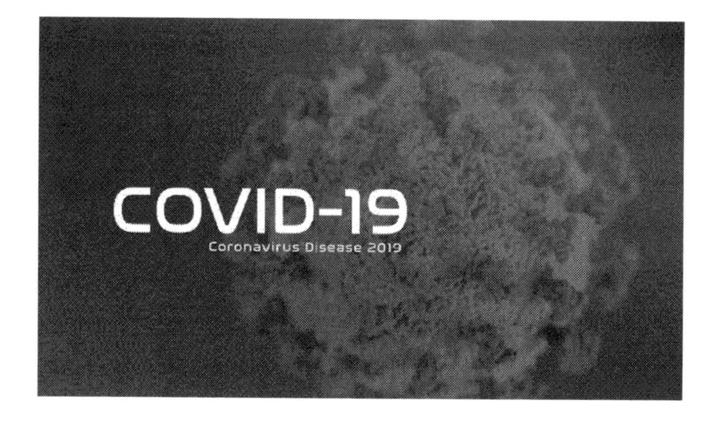

#1 Stay clean and healthy by ditching your shoes at the door.

Before you enter your home take your shoes off outside or in the entryway then wear your indoor shoes in the home.

#2 Change your gloves often as more families go back and forth from school and work. It is even more important to keep gloves and masks clean. Wash your reusable ones and get new disposable ones every day.

#3 Change your bed sheets every week. Bed sheets are a surface many people forget about but keeping them clean prevents a buildup of bacteria and germs from sitting there each night.

Tip #16

Bathroom sweeps in 10 minutes or less…

There are a lot of things in your bathroom that might block you or create a barrier while cleaning, like shampoo bottles, soap, brushes, etc. Remove them and keep them aside in a bucket or wherever you feel comfortable. Also keep all the other things like stools, clothes, slippers, etc. out of the bathroom. This will make your job go quickly.

Water spots are unavoidable at places where water is constantly flowing. For example, shower, sink, etc. To remove them rub lemon over the area where you find water spots. The citric acid present in the lemon acts as a good antibacterial cleaner. This will easily remove those spots and take care of the unwanted smell as well. Still, if you are not able to get these spots, apply some shaving cream or soap and then clean it.

Toilets...

Basically, it's just not the toilet seat that is dirty, it is the whole toilet set! The first thing you need to do is dust the toilet and then clean its surface.

The second step is to clean the toilet thoroughly to get rid of the germs. For that, you need borax and vinegar. Pour the borax and vinegar into the toilet and let it sit for some time. Flush after 15 minutes for a "germ-free" toilet.

I would like to share one of my personal experiences where I flushed the remaining cold drinks into the toilet. The next day when I went to use my washroom it was sparkling clean. Not kidding, it was shining. I would recommend using the leftover aerated drinks at your house party to get a sparkling white toilet. Cleaning was never so easy, what do you think?

Mirrors...

Black tea should be used to get the desired results on your mirror (s). It is one of the best mirror cleaners around the house and using it is simple.

Filter the tea leaves and pour the remaining black tea into a sprayer. Spray the black tea on the mirror and let it sit for a few seconds. Spray clean water and clean the mirror with a cloth.

Again, lemon is a great cleaning agent. For cleaning, you must follow simple steps. First cut the lemon into two halves and clean the whole sink including the tap with it.

How to stay in contact with me:

Clean it Best, LLC

Letscleanupyourmess.com

IG: @wecleanitbest

FB: @cleanitbest

Made in the USA
Middletown, DE
03 October 2023